MY FIRST BOOK of NATURE

Camilla
de la Bedoyere

Jane
Newland

templar
books

CONTENTS

Plants

Bugs

LADYBIRD HUNT

Can you find the ladybirds hiding in this book? There is one in every scene, all except one.

Go to page 63 to find out.

Birds

Animals

Plants

Oak

Sweet pea

Rose

Bird of paradise flower

Pitcher plant

Dandelion

Cactus

Scots pine

Apple blossom

Vine

Sunflower

Palm

Giant sequoia

Fern

Orchid

Daisy

THE STORY OF A SEED

A seed holds new life inside, and with warmth, air and water it can grow into a new plant. This is how a broad bean plant grows from a little seed.

Plants need sunlight to grow

Corn kernel

Avocado stone

Sycamore seed

Seeds can be tiny or as big as your head. Many are round, some are flat and others have wings.

Burr

Mountain laurel seed

Poppy seeds

④ More and more leaves shoot out as the plant grows tall and strong.

③ A green shoot grows up towards the light. Two little leaves unfurl and open.

② The seed's case cracks open and a white root grows down. It sucks up water from the soil.

New roots grow longer and fatter

① A seed falls onto the ground or it is buried.

First root

It's damp and dark in the soil

Growing plants need plenty of water

Broad bean plant

(5)

Flower buds appear, and burst into colourful petals.

Purple flowers

Hungry snails munch on the sweet juicy leaves of young plants

The plant's roots keep on growing. They hold the seedling in the ground so it doesn't fall over.

ALL ABOUT FLOWERS

A huge golden sunflower lifts its face to the sun and shows off its petals. It has an important job to do and it needs the help of some buzzing bees. Flowers make seeds.

① The sunflower's sweet smell and yellow petals attract bees.

A sunflower head has lots of tiny flowers in its centre

② A bee sips the sugary nectar inside the flower and brushes against a yellow powder called pollen.

③ The bee flies from flower to flower looking for nectar to drink.

Most plants have flowers, and many of them are big and colourful with a sweet smell.

Rose

Daffodil

Daisy

5

Now, the sunflower begins to change. Each tiny flower grows into a seed.

A goldfinch perches on the sunflower to eat the tasty seeds

4

When the bee lands on another flower, some pollen falls off. This is called pollination.

Foxglove

Pollen dust sticks to a bee's furry body

Passionflower

Lily

11

NATURE'S HARVEST

Fruits and vegetables grow in all sorts of shapes, sizes and colours. Some vegetables are hidden underground, but many fruits grow high up in the trees. They are food for lots of animals — including us!

A vegetable is any part of a plant that is good to eat, from leafy green shoots to plump roots.

This pea pod has just popped!

Carrots, potatoes, yams and beets are some of the vegetables that grow in the soil, or just at its surface.

Peas and beans grow inside a pod. When the pod pops open, they are scattered around and will grow in new places.

Radish

Beetroot

Lettuce

A carrot is a thick orange root

Potatoes

These vegetables are ready to be dug up!

Oranges, lemons, limes and grapefruits are citrus fruits. They have thick skin and juicy insides high in vitamin C.

Lemons

Bananas grow in bunches

A fruit is the part of a plant that grows around a seed. As fruits ripen in the hot summer sun, they grow sweeter.

Grapes are berries

A berry is a fruit with seeds inside. A tomato is a berry with lots of seeds, but a cranberry has just four.

Tropical fruits, such as bananas and pineapples, grow in hot places where there is sunshine and rain all year round.

Rambutans

A pumpkin is a type of vegetable called a squash

Pink dragon fruit

Pineapple

BEWARE!
Some fruits and vegetables must be cooked before they are eaten. Never eat any part of a plant unless an adult tells you it's safe.

TOWERING TREES

Trees grow tall and strong, raising their leaves high into the sky where the sun shines brightest. They can be found all over the world, except where it's very cold or very hot.

Oak tree in winter

Oak tree in summer

Scots pine

When summer ends, broadleaf trees such as oaks drop their leaves. In spring, they will burst into life again.

Acorns

Pine cones

Larches are conifers, but their needles change colour and fall in the autumn

Tall, spindly conifer trees, like Scots pines, grow in cool places. They keep their needle-like leaves all year, and their seeds grow in cones.

One tree ring shows one year of growth. How old do you think this tree is?

The Cedar of Lebanon is sturdy and stout with wide-reaching branches. It grows on steep mountainsides and can live for hundreds of years.

Cedar of Lebanon

Baobab tree

Tall baobabs are called upside-down trees! When it rains they store the water in their fat trunks.

Coconut palm

Conifer trees are also called evergreens

Mango tree

A palm tree unfurls its big leafy fronds from the top of its trunk. Tree ferns look like small palm trees.

Tree fern

Mango fruit

The branches of fruit trees may bend and droop, but they are strong enough to hold hundreds of plump fruits.

ALL KINDS OF LEAVES

From prickly cactus spines to huge fan-shaped fronds, leaves are working hard all the time. A leaf is the place where a plant makes its food.

Needle-shaped

Most leaves are broad and flat, so they can catch lots of sunlight. They come in many different shapes, but there are five main types.

Lots of animals eat leaves as food. Clever orangutans use them to build nests and to scoop up water to drink.

Big leaves can be useful as umbrellas for orangutans!

Barrel cactus

Oval-shaped

Long

Hand-shaped

Compound
(many leaves on one stem)

Plants make food in a special
way called photosynthesis
(foh-toh-sin-the-sis).

② Air is sucked into leaves through
tiny holes in their surface

① Sunlight passes
into leaves

Prickly
pear cactus

④ Leaves use sunlight to turn
the air and water into food

③ Water travels from the soil into the
roots, up the stem to the leaves

Rabbits eat juicy
grass stems

Cacti grow in hot deserts.
Their stems are fat and swollen
with water and their leaves grow
as spines. These prickles stop
animals nibbling them!

The thick, flat leaves of a
stone plant look like pebbles

17

THE RAINFOREST

A rainforest is full of lush, big-leaved plants and towering trees. It rains most days, but it is always hot. Plants like warmth and water, so it's a perfect place for them to grow.

Tree branches create a thick layer of leaves called the canopy

Titan arum and rafflesia (raf-lee-see-a) are huge stinky flowers that grow on the forest floor. Their bad smell attracts flies and other insects.

The long stems of vines dangle from branches

The titan arum's flower is taller than a person!

Below the canopy, palms, ferns, bushes and young trees fight for sunlight

Rafflesia flowers grow to one metre across

Animals, from tigers and hanging sloths to ants and tiny hummingbirds, make their homes in rainforests.

The tallest trees poke out above the canopy

A hummingbird hovers to sip a flower's sweet nectar

Lobster claw flower

Orchid

Some flowers don't need soil at all. Plants like this orchid grow high up on tree branches. Their roots dangle in the damp air.

Colourful mushrooms grow on the ground, where it's gloomy and wet.

Mushrooms

19

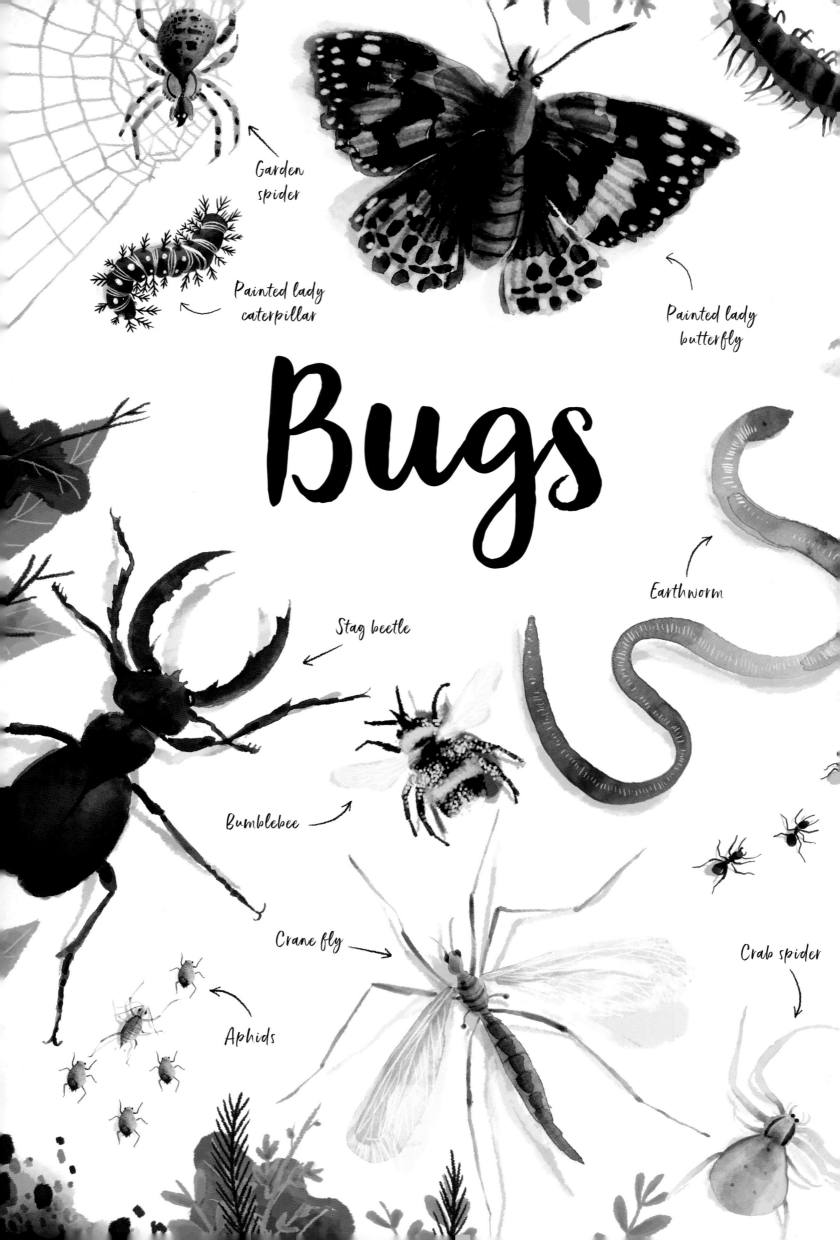

Garden spider

Painted lady caterpillar

Painted lady butterfly

Bugs

Earthworm

Stag beetle

Bumblebee

Crane fly

Aphids

Crab spider

Centipede

Emperor dragonfly

Orchid mantis

Woodlouse

Cuckoo wasp

Black ants

Shield bug

Garden snail

Blow fly

Ladybird

Bella moth

Short-horned grasshopper

Scarab beetle

Stick insect

Bella moth caterpillar

BUG FIGHT!

It's a bug-eat-bug world out there. When bugs are not hunting for food, they're being hunted as food! These crawly critters have some clever ways to catch a meal and avoid attack.

A hornet gives a nasty sting

Yellow and black stripes warn of danger. Most stripy bugs have a sting in their tail.

Many-legged centipedes and speedy tiger beetles can run fast to chase down prey

An army of driver ants is on the march. They work as a team to attack other animals. Big ants, called soldiers, guard the smaller workers.

Soldier ants have large mouthparts to grab and bite

Assassin bugs inject a liquid that turns other bugs to juice!

Orchid mantis

An orchid mantis looks like a pink flower. When another bug comes near it will shoot its spiny front legs forwards in a split-second to grab its meal.

Blackbird

Monarch caterpillars munch on milkweed leaves so that they taste bad to hungry birds

A harmless hoverfly looks like a stinging bug

All of these bugs are masters of trickery. They stay out of danger by pretending to be something else.

A thorn bug pretends to be a prickly thorn

Spicebush swallowtail caterpillars look like mini snakes

A katydid may lose a leg in a fight so it can get away

Click beetles can flick their bodies high into the air

Grasshoppers and click beetles both have the same idea when escaping danger – to jump up and away.

Grasshoppers have long, springy legs for leaping to safety

Bombardier beetle

Beware a fearsome bombardier beetle – it defends itself by spraying a stinging liquid from its bottom!

23

A TIME TO CHANGE

Caterpillars are baby bugs that look very different from the moths and butterflies they change into. This is the life cycle of the monarch butterfly.

When caterpillars turn into butterflies they go through a big change called a metamorphosis (meta-morf-o-sis).

④ The caterpillar makes a hard case, called a chrysalis (kris-uh-lis), around its body.

③ Caterpillars eat and eat and eat! They need to grow fat before they can change.

The caterpillar's stripy skin warns birds that it is poisonous

Chrysalis

② The eggs hatch and little caterpillars appear.

Eggs

① A female butterfly lays her tiny eggs on the underside of a leaf, where birds can't see them.

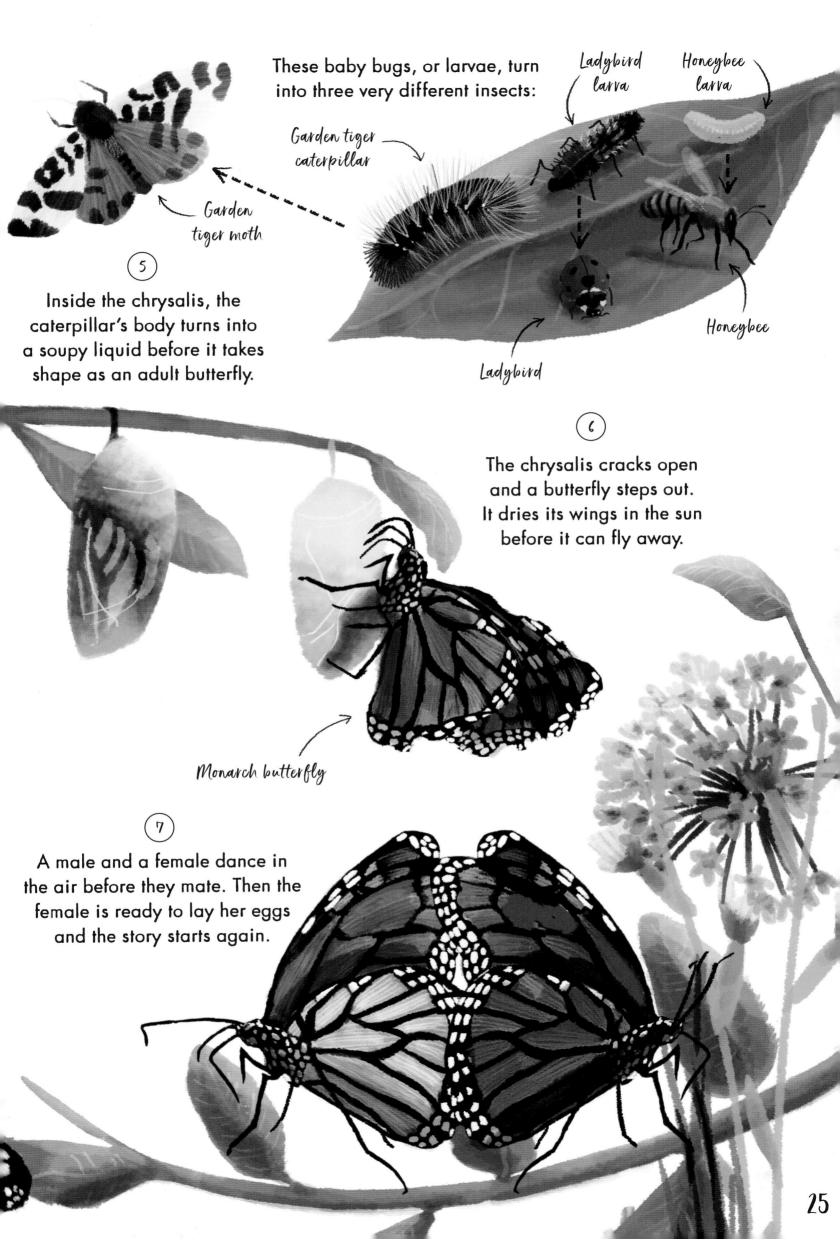

These baby bugs, or larvae, turn into three very different insects:

Ladybird larva

Honeybee larva

Garden tiger caterpillar

Garden tiger moth

Ladybird

Honeybee

5

Inside the chrysalis, the caterpillar's body turns into a soupy liquid before it takes shape as an adult butterfly.

6

The chrysalis cracks open and a butterfly steps out. It dries its wings in the sun before it can fly away.

Monarch butterfly

7

A male and a female dance in the air before they mate. Then the female is ready to lay her eggs and the story starts again.

I SPY A SPIDER

Most bugs have six legs, but spiders have eight. They can run speedily, build traps and spin silken webs. They are the superheroes of the bug world.

Spiders hunt other bugs to eat. They have strong jaws and sharp fangs to bite and inject deadly venom.

Spinnerets, where silk is made

Body

Eight legs

Head with fangs

① A spider spins silk in a Y-shape between twigs, to make a frame.

② Strong silk threads are added to the edges.

③ A sticky silk is used to spin a spiral, starting from the middle.

Fly

④ Hiding close by, a spider waits for a bug to fly into its web.

Many spiders build webs from silk that they make in their spinnerets. They use webs to trap food.

Spiders have huge brains for their body size, and some clever abilities, too. Spiders have super sight – they can have up to 12 eyes, and super senses – they can smell, hear and taste with their feet!

Desert spiders get around by cartwheeling, so their feet don't get burnt on the hot sand

Supermum wolf spiders carry hundreds of babies on their back to keep them safe

The colourful peacock spider can jump high into the air

A net-casting spider hangs on a thread. It holds a stretchy web in its legs, ready to catch a woodlouse!

Net-casting spider

Trapdoor spiders build a silk door over their burrow entrance, then cover it with soil to make the trap almost invisible.

Trapdoor spider

27

POND BUGS

Beneath the shimmering surface of ponds and rivers there is a hidden underwater world of bugs. Here, they can find a home, food and plenty of places to hide.

Adult mayflies live for just a few days

A blue and green emperor dragonfly darts about above a pond. It started its life in the water.

Emperor dragonfly

④

A nymph moults up to 10 times before it climbs out of the water and becomes an adult.

①

A dragonfly lays her eggs at the water's surface and sticks them to a plant stem.

Nymphs can spend up to five years underwater

③

As a nymph grows it sheds its old skin. This is called moulting.

②

After a few weeks the eggs hatch into tiny, wriggly babies called nymphs.

Frogs lay hundreds of soft eggs, called frogspawn, in the water

Frogspawn

Pond worms can breathe underwater

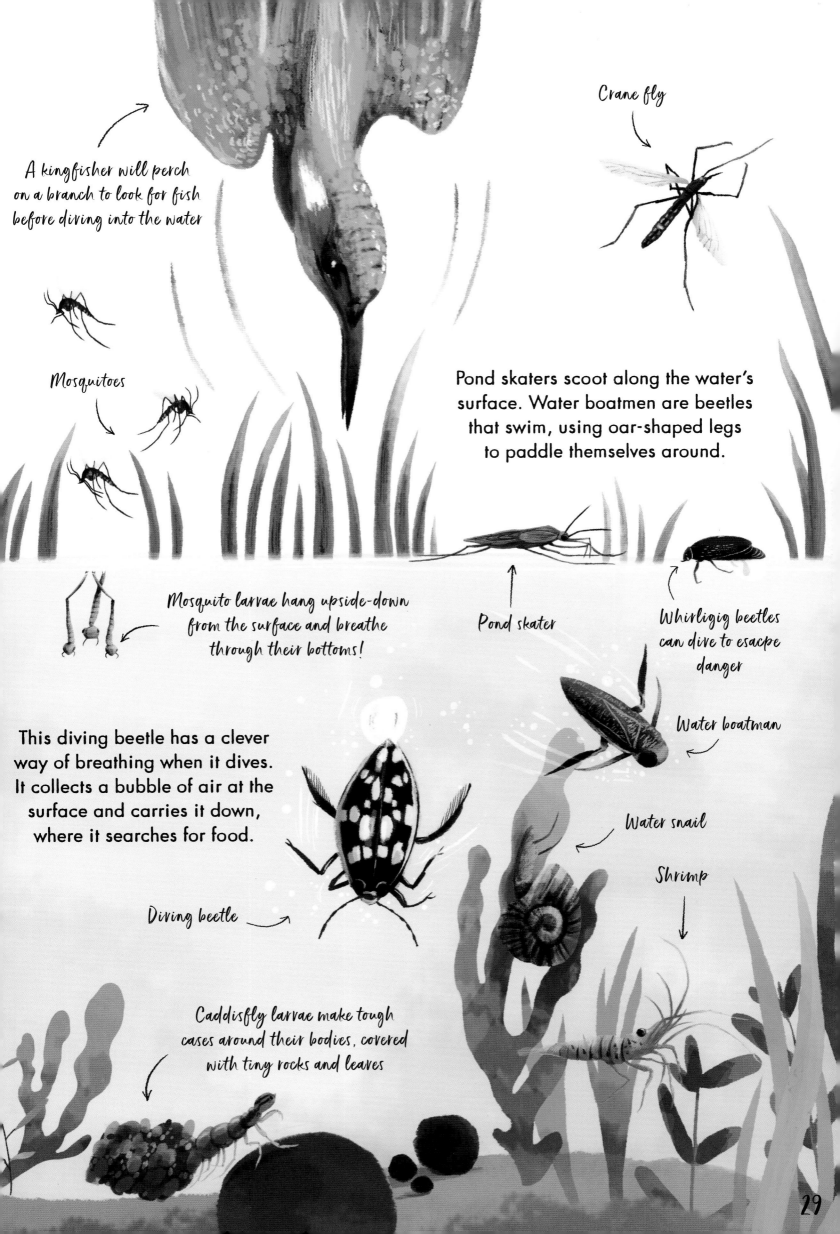

A kingfisher will perch on a branch to look for fish before diving into the water

Crane fly

Mosquitoes

Pond skaters scoot along the water's surface. Water boatmen are beetles that swim, using oar-shaped legs to paddle themselves around.

Mosquito larvae hang upside-down from the surface and breathe through their bottoms!

Pond skater

Whirligig beetles can dive to esacpe danger

Water boatman

This diving beetle has a clever way of breathing when it dives. It collects a bubble of air at the surface and carries it down, where it searches for food.

Water snail

Shrimp

Diving beetle

Caddisfly larvae make tough cases around their bodies, covered with tiny rocks and leaves

GOING UNDERGROUND

Millions of bugs are busy beneath our feet. They lurk under stones, tunnel through soft soil and munch through piles of old, rotting leaves.

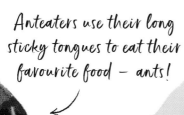

Anteaters use their long sticky tongues to eat their favourite food – ants!

Ants store dead leaves and eat the mould that grows on them

It's all action in an ant nest! Thousands of tiny bugs scurry along tunnels, carrying food, eggs and leaves to different rooms, called chambers.

Worm cast

Ant graveyard

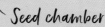

Seed chamber

Earthworm

Worker ants dig new tunnels and chambers

Larvae chamber

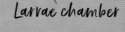

Pupae chamber

Centipedes and millipedes have long, thin bodies – perfect for tunnelling

Only the queen ant lays eggs

Earthworms eat soil as they burrow through it

Centipede

Egg chamber

A tunnel is a safe place for worms and other creepy-crawlies to hide out. It's damp and cool and there is always something to eat.

③ Males begin to 'sing' to females.

④ After mating, females lay eggs in tree bark.

② They moult and turn into adults. They wait for their soft skin to turn hard and strong.

⑤ When new nymphs hatch they fall to the ground.

① Cicada nymphs come out of the ground and climb a tree trunk.

When earwigs, slugs and other bugs are not hiding in tunnels and burrows, they live among dead leaves and twigs, called leaf litter.

Woodlice

Earwig

⑥ They burrow into the ground to find tree roots.

Bumblebees sleep underground in the winter

The nymphs of cicadas live underground for up to 17 years. Here, they feed on the juice of tree roots.

Larvae

Lots of bugs lay their eggs below ground, safe from hungry birds

When it gets too hot, slugs disappear into the soil

Some scorpions only come out of their burrow at night

31

BIG BUGS

Meet the incredible creepy-crawlies that hold the record for being the longest, heaviest or biggest. These are supersized bugs!

The weta is a plant-eating monster bug that looks like a plump grasshopper. The biggest wetas are some of the heaviest insects in the world.

Tarantula hawk wasp

Tarantula hawk wasps measure up to 5 centimetres long but they can defeat tarantulas the size of dinner plates!

A giant weta weighs about the same as an apple

The goliath beetle's flying wings are covered by a hard red wing case

The goliath beetle is the world's biggest insect at 11.5 centimetres long. This big bug is so strong it can lift more than 850 times its own weight!

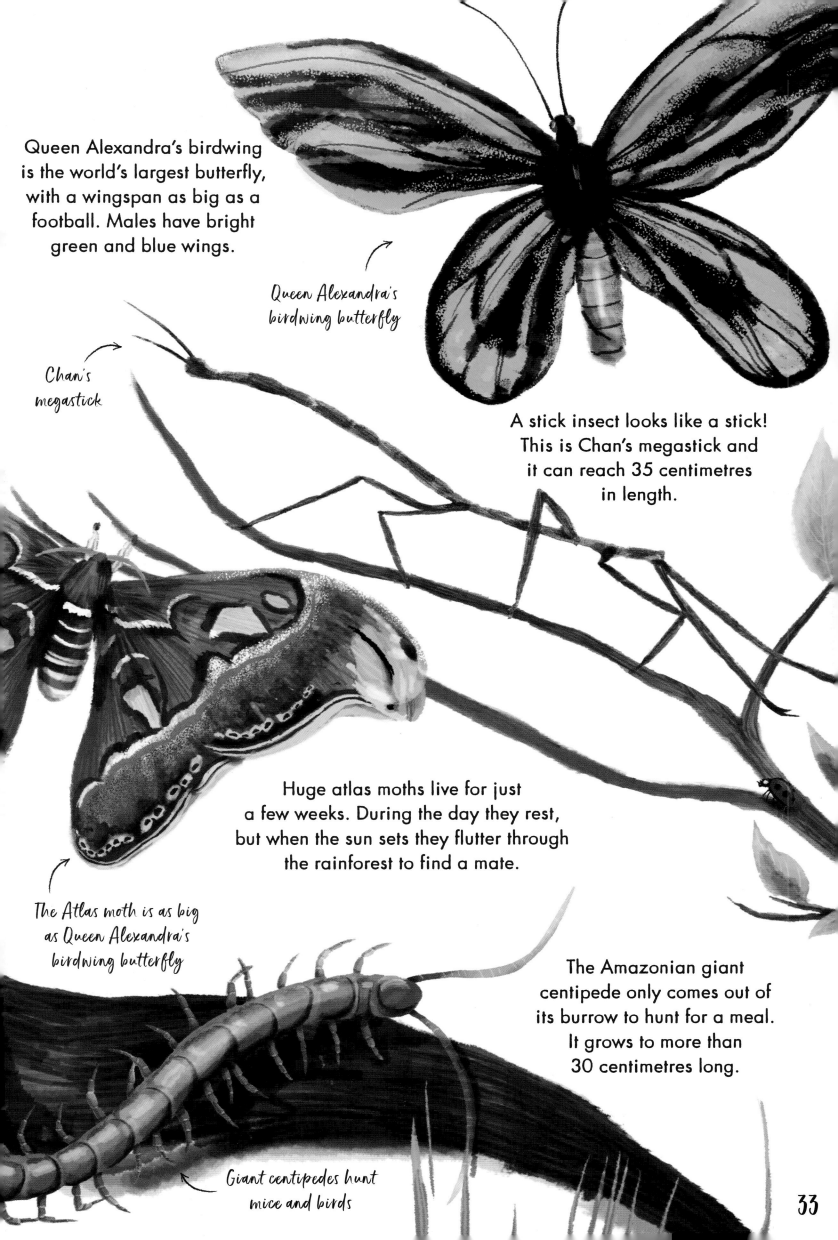

Queen Alexandra's birdwing is the world's largest butterfly, with a wingspan as big as a football. Males have bright green and blue wings.

Queen Alexandra's birdwing butterfly

Chan's megastick

A stick insect looks like a stick! This is Chan's megastick and it can reach 35 centimetres in length.

Huge atlas moths live for just a few weeks. During the day they rest, but when the sun sets they flutter through the rainforest to find a mate.

The Atlas moth is as big as Queen Alexandra's birdwing butterfly

The Amazonian giant centipede only comes out of its burrow to hunt for a meal. It grows to more than 30 centimetres long.

Giant centipedes hunt mice and birds

33

Nightingale

Puffin

Hummingbird

Lovebird

Birds

Northern cardinal

Stork

Flamingo

Ostrich

Oystercatcher

Blue-footed booby

Canada geese

Raggiana bird
of paradise

Barn owl

Peacock

African grey
parrot

Chicken

Duck

Macaroni
penguin

ALL ABOUT BIRDS

Some birds fly far and high over land and sea and others are fast runners and swift swimmers. There are 10,000 different kinds of bird in the world.

A swallow is an expert flier

Birds are the only animals that have feathers. A bird also has a beak, no teeth, two legs and two wings.

Few animals can travel the world as easily as a bird. By flapping its wings, a bird can take to the air.

Eye

Song thrush

Wing

Beak

Belly

Tail

Feet with claws

A bird's feathers keep it warm and help it to fly. These are the main types.

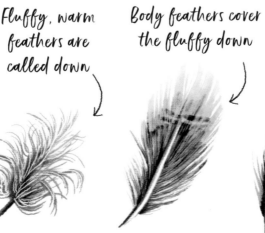

Fluffy, warm feathers are called down

Body feathers cover the fluffy down

Long flight feathers grow on the wings

Tail feather

A coot has wide toes for walking on floating leaves

Birds of prey have sharp claws called talons

A stork's long toes help it to walk across muddy marshes

A duck's webbed feet are like paddles

Ostriches have large padded feet for running

A bird's foot is just right for its way of life. Strong toes and claws help a bird to perch on a branch or to grab on to prey and webbed feet are great for swimming.

A toucan's huge beak can reach fruit at the tips of branches

A bird of prey uses its strong hooked beak to grip small animals

A heron's long, slender beak is perfect for grabbing slippery fish

A bird's beak can tell us a lot about the food it eats. Each is the perfect shape for their favourite type of food.

EGGS AND CHICKS

All birds lay eggs and most birds build nests. Parents take care of their eggs until they hatch. They feed and protect their chicks and teach them how to find their own food.

Female ostrich

Male ostrich

Long-legged ostriches are the tallest birds in the world. They are too big to fly but they can run very fast.

Ostriches live in Africa

A male ostrich has made a nest on the ground and a female has laid her eggs inside. She sits on the eggs to keep them warm, and the male will help out too.

Ostrich egg (15 cm)

Emu egg (13 cm)

Goose egg (9 cm)

Chicken egg (6 cm)

Quail egg (2.5 cm)

A weaver bird's nest hangs from a branch

Hummingbirds build the smallest nests

A nest is a safe place for a bird to keep its eggs. Birds build cosy nests in branches, in tree holes, on the side of cliffs or on the ground.

A swallow's nest is made from mud and spit

Baby birds learn how to find food by copying their parents. Ostriches eat seeds, flowers, grass and bugs.

Chicks stay close for safety

Fluffy ostrich chicks hatch from their eggs after 40 days, ready to walk. They leave the nest within a few days.

A baby bird grows inside an egg. All the food it needs is inside it too. Some birds lay one egg at a time, but quails lay more than 20!

Newly hatched ostrich chicks can be as big as chickens

HUNGRY BIRDS

Birds eat all kinds of food. They don't have teeth, so they usually swallow food whole and then grind it up in their stomachs. Flying and building nests is hard work, so a bird is always hungry!

Gannet

A fresh fish!

Gannets will fly for hours, searching the sea for any signs of fish. When a gannet spots a meal it dives head first into the water to grab it.

A flamingo's feathers turn pink because it eats pink food

A bee-eater catches a flying bug. It throws the bug up in the air and swallows it in one big gulp.

Bee-eaters eat bees and dragonflies

A flamingo eats by hanging its head upside-down in water. It uses its big beak to scoop up water, then it filters out tiny shrimps using its comblike tongue.

Birds of prey hunt animals to eat. They are fast, strong birds that have very good eyesight and large clawed feet called talons. Owls, eagles and falcons are birds of prey.

Barn owl

Soft wing feathers mean an owl can fly silently

A sharp, hooked beak can tear up food easily

Strong, clawed feet can hold onto wriggly prey

This snail kite has caught its dinner. It will use its perfectly hooked bill to pull the snail's soft body out of its shell.

The hoatzin is one of the smelliest birds!

The snail kite is named after its favourite food

Hoatzins are the only birds that eat leaves. A leaf doesn't have much goodness in it, so hoatzins spend a lot of time eating!

PENGUINS

The freezing Antarctic at the South Pole is home to millions of strange birds called penguins. In winter, Emperor penguins gather on the ice to find mates.

Penguins waddle or belly-slide across the ice

APRIL
Winter is coming and the sea is turning to ice. Emperor penguins have been fishing in the sea, but now they swim to land.

Mother birds walk back to the sea to fish while the fathers look after the eggs

Thousands of birds gather in a group called a colony

Father penguin

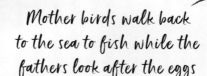

MAY
A mother penguin lays one egg and the father carefully places it on his feet. His soft belly feathers cover the egg and keep it warm.

NOVEMBER
The whole family returns to the sea to enjoy the short Antarctic summer.

There are 17 different types of penguin. The emperor is the biggest. These others live on islands around the Antarctic.

Macaroni

Chinstrap

Gentoo

Narwhal

Chicks can't swim until their black and white feathers have fully grown

Mother penguin

AUGUST
The mothers return with food for the new chicks. Both parents look after the chick as it grows bigger and stronger.

A fluffy coat of soft, grey feathers helps to keep chicks warm on the ice

JULY
After 70 days the egg hatches. A cold wind blows, bringing blizzards of snow. The fathers and chicks have not eaten for two months.

43

SONG AND DANCE

Many birds talk to each other by singing. They may also flick their colourful feathers and perform dances to show how they are feeling.

A male nightingale sings a beautiful song to attract a female

Birds make different sounds, from hoots to cheeps and tweets. Baby songbirds start to learn their songs from their parents at just 10 days old.

A male lyrebird sings and shakes its long tail feathers to impress a mate

Bitterns have a loud, deep booming call. Their song can be heard up to 5 kilometres away, making it the loudest bird of all.

Bittern

African grey parrot

African grey parrots are copycats. They mimic the songs of other birds they hear in their rainforest home.

Two cranes perform a bird ballet that can last for hours. The courting pair move together, bowing, leaping and flapping their wings.

Raggiana bird of paradise

Japanese cranes clatter their beaks together

A male blue-footed booby impresses his mate by showing her his lovely blue feet. The bluer they are, the more attractive she thinks he is!

Birds of paradise are the superstars of the bird world. Males have fancy feathers in bright colours and they show them off in dazzling dances.

Blue-footed booby

45

WATER BIRDS

Many types of bird live near water, because there is plenty of food to feast on. Huge seabirds soar over the blue oceans and slender-legged wading birds feed on small animals at the shore.

Heron

Storks find fish, frogs and worms to eat in shallow water

Rivers, lakes and marshes are home to birds with long legs and big feet – just right for wading through water and mud.

The strange-looking shoebill has spied a fish in the murky water

Baby swans are called cygnets

Puffins nest on cliffs, and fly out over the ocean to catch fish

Black-headed gull

Oystercatchers use their pointed beak to pick worms and shellfish from the sand

The shallow water where the sea meets the land is home to many sea creatures, such as fish and crabs, all tempting to hungry waterbirds.

A pelican's huge beak can scoop up a mouthful of fish

Petrel

Albatrosses can glide for hours on their huge wings

Birds that live at sea have long, broad wings for soaring over the water – often for weeks at a time. They dive into the water when they spot something to eat.

Penguins use their flipper-like wings to fly through the water to chase fish

47

Lar gibbon

Warthog

Giraffe

Animals

Ring-tailed lemur

Capybara

Arctic hare

Jerboa

Tiger

Poison dart frog

Red squirrel

Marmot

Rhino

Bat

Lioness
and cubs

Yellow
eyelash
viper

Reindeer

Tapir

Chameleon

Fennec fox

Gorilla

Mouse

HIDE AND SEEK

With no fur or feathers, amphibians and reptiles have slimy or scaly skins. Bright colours and bold patterns help them hide from hungry predators or show off to mates!

Chameleons are lizards, and many are green so they can hide amongst the leaves of their rainforest home. But when they get excited, their skin turns a rainbow of colours!

A chameleon's long sticky tongue . . .

. . . is perfect for catching flies

This amphibian wants to be seen! A poison dart frog's bold colours warn other animals that its slimy skin is covered in poison.

Strawberry poison dart frog

A horned frog looks like a brown leaf on the forest floor, because its colour and body shape help it to blend in. This is called camouflage.

Horned frog

Snakes are reptiles with long bodies that can slither silently to sneak up on prey. Many snakes have a deadly bite, and all swallow their food whole.

This yellow eyelash viper likes to hide amongst bananas

Emerald tree boas are hard to spot in the leaves

Young eastern newts live on land and their skin is bright orange. Adults live in ponds, and turn greeny brown to hide from predators.

Young eastern newt

Crocodile

Crocodiles lurk in rivers and swamps. They swim along slowly with just their eyes and nostrils above the water, keeping a lookout for their next meal.

51

FAMILY LIFE

Monkeys and apes are mammals that are found in forests in warm places. They live in friendly family groups, taking care of each other and looking after the babies.

A spider monkey calls to other monkeys to tell them there's food to eat

Spider monkeys live in big groups. They love hanging from branches and leaping through the trees. Their long, gripping tail helps them to get around.

A male gorilla is called a silverback

Gorillas are the largest apes. They are too heavy to climb trees, so a family builds a soft bed of leaves on the ground.

Gibbons have long arms to swing through the trees. At sunrise, males and females call to each other in a chorus of loud hoots.

Lar gibbon

Mother and father golden lion tamarins take turns to look after their babies. These small monkeys get their name from the fur growing around their faces.

Like all monkeys and apes, tamarins stroke and clean each other's fur

One hundred chimpanzees can be in one family group. These apes eat fruits, nuts and insects, and they have learnt some clever ways to get at them.

Chimps use rocks to crack open tough nuts

Ring-tailed lemurs search on the ground for fruit, leaves and flowers to eat. They hold their tails up high so they can see each other.

Ring-tailed lemurs

ANIMAL HOMES

An animal's home is called a habitat. From snow-covered mountaintops to sun-scorched deserts, animals can make a place to live almost anywhere on Earth.

A thick layer of fat helps seals keep warm

Reindeer snuffle in the snow to find plants beneath it

Polar bear

Arctic fox

An Arctic hare's fur turns from brown to white in winter

In the polar lands at the far ends of the Earth, the winter is long and very cold. Many animals have warm white coats that camouflage them.

Mountain goats clamber up and down the steep slopes

Bald eagle

On steep, rocky mountaintops, few trees and plants grow and the weather can change quickly. Animals that live here must be tough and sure-footed.

Alpine marmots live in cosy burrows

A bobcat's spotty coat helps it blend into its rocky home

A desert is a hot, dry place that gets almost no rain. Few plants can grow, but there are some amazing animals that have adapted to survive in the heat.

An Arabian oryx can go without water for weeks

A fennec fox's big ears can hear beetles in the sand

Dromedary camels store water as fat in their hump

Jerboas leap across the hot sand on their kangaroo-like legs

Spotty jaguars prowl and hunt in the leafy shadows

Toucan

Sloths hang from branches all day long

Tropical rainforests are warm and rainy. From the bottom of a river to the tops of the trees, animals find places to hunt, hide and relax.

Tapir

Tapirs and capybaras feed on fruits, shoots and berries, often near water

Capybara

THE AFRICAN SAVANNAH

The savannah is a special habitat in Africa where grass grows on vast plains. Herds of grazing animals munch the grass, but there are some hungry predators here, too.

Flying vultures look out for food

Herd of wildebeest

Little rain falls for half the year, so herd animals, such as wildebeest, journey to other places to find water and food. When the rains come again, the grass grows back and the animals return.

Giraffes

Zebra

Hippos

Waterhole

Male lion

Rhino

Lioness and cubs

Gaboon viper

Lions live in family groups called prides. The male looks after his pride and will fight other lions that come close. The lioness does the hunting, so she can feed her cubs when they are hungry.

Dung beetle

A huge grassland is called a savannah in
Africa, a pampas in South America, a prairie
in North America and a steppe in Russia.
Few big trees grow because there is little rain.

Termite
mounds

Herds of antelope
and elephants roam the
grassland. They stay
together for safety while
they graze on plants.

Leopard

Antelope

Elephants

Vultures

Crocodile

Acacia tree

Weaver
bird nest

Weaver bird

Little yellow weaver birds
dart between trees. They
weave their hanging
nests from grass.

Warthog

OCEAN WORLD

The underwater habitat that lies beneath the surface of the ocean is home to the largest animal to ever live, millions of fish and lots of other incredible creatures.

Sea grass

Green turtle

Most of the life in the ocean can be found in the shallow, sunlit parts, from corals and turtles, to whales and colourful fish.

Regal angelfish

Huge green turtles come to seagrass meadows to feed. Swaying seagrasses grow in the clear, shallow water at the coast.

Seahorse

Blacktip reef shark

Tiny animals called polyps build rocky reefs. A coral reef is full of food and hiding places, so many animals make it their home.

Clownfish

A coral reef is a rainbow of colour

Red Pacific octopus

Seabirds soar above the waves, watching for fish and jellyfish

Flying fish use their fins like wings to leap out of the water

Mackerel

Dolphins work together to hunt for fish. A group of silvery mackerel dive, twist and turn as they try to escape.

Bottlenose dolphin

The humpback isn't the biggest whale but it can grow longer than a bus!

Mauve stinger jellyfish

Deep-sea vent

Yeti crabs

In the deep, deep sea, there is no sunlight. Steam gushes from deep-sea vents on the seabed, and it turns the water into a boiling bubbly bath for the strange-looking animals that live there.

Anglerfish

Tube worms

IN THE NIGHTTIME

Sleep is important for all animals. Unlike us, many creatures stir at night and rest during the day. Others spend weeks, or even months, fast asleep!

Animals that use the cover of darkness to eat, hunt or find mates are called nocturnal animals.

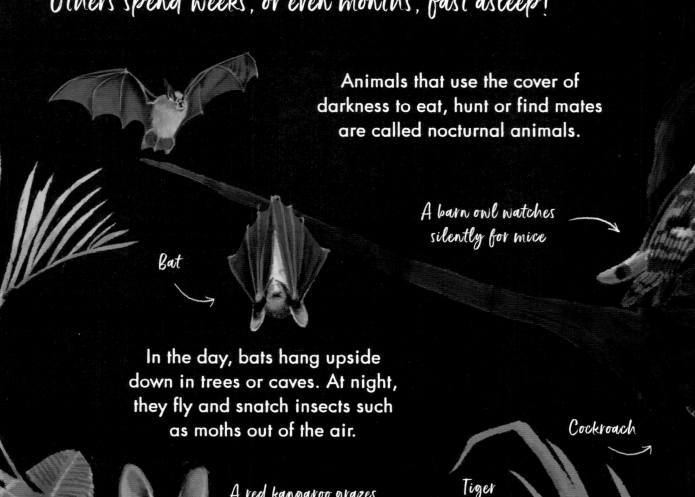

A barn owl watches silently for mice

Bat

In the day, bats hang upside down in trees or caves. At night, they fly and snatch insects such as moths out of the air.

Cockroach

A red kangaroo grazes at night when it's cool

Tiger

Aardvarks sniff out ants in the dark

Mouse

This red squirrel has stayed up late to collect nuts

Bat

Twinkling fireflies are little bugs that make light in their bottoms. At night they flash to one another through the moonlit forest.

Fireflies

Some animals sleep for many months. In places where winters are long and harsh, some animals would struggle to survive. So they snuggle up in a cosy bed and wait for spring to arrive. A long winter sleep is called hibernation.

Bear and cubs

Some bears, tortoises and rabbits settle down for a deep sleep until spring.

Tortoise

Rabbits come out of their burrows at sunrise and sunset

NATURE WORDS

AMPHIBIAN
An animal with slimy, wet skin that can live on land and in water.

BUG
Any small, boneless animal, such as a slug, spider or fly, that lives on land.

CAMOUFLAGE
How some animals blend into their habitat.

DECIDUOUS
A type of tree that drops its leaves each autumn.

EGG
An object laid by female animals, such as birds, that has a baby inside.

EVERGREEN
A type of tree that keeps its leaves all year.

HIBERNATION
A time of long rest during the winter.

INSECT
A small, boneless animal that has six legs and three body segments. Some have wings.

LARVA
A baby insect.

MAMMAL
An animal that normally gives birth to live babies and feeds them with milk.

MATING
When a male and a female meet to make babies.

MOULT
When a bug loses its old skin to grow bigger.